This book belongs to

_____

Roses are Red and I'm Farting Fred

Humor Heals Us

Roses are red,
And I'm farting Fred.
Today is the day
I totally dread.

The girl next door,
She wants a kiss.
If it was up to me,
I'd give Valentine's Day a miss!

Why doesn't she like
Burping Bryce down the street.
He may burp a lot,
But he dresses real neat.

Here's pooting Pete,
My best friend ever.
He wants us to
Go out sledding, together.

Pete said he got me
A cool snow sled.
So down the long road,
We swiftly sped.

Our farts helped propel us,
And made us go fast.
I don't want to admit it,
But I'm having a blast.

Woosh! Past the Acropolis
We go.
Look! There's the Parthenon
Down below.

Our gas carries us
Up the Eiffel Tower,
Then past the Arc de Triomphe
With full fart power.

These amazing places...
We got to see 'em.
We even got
To see the Colosseum.

Hello, Leaning Tower of Pisa!
And Goodbye!
There's Buckingham Palace
As we fly by.

Thank goodness
I ate my fiber today.
The tourists at the Great Wall
Are singing away.

Mount Fuji is so tall.
It can't be missed.
And the Taj Mahal has always been
On my bucket list.

Pete's gas fuels the trip,
But it totally stinks!
It's so awaesome
To see the Great Sphinx.

I'm feeling so dizzy.
I might pass out soon,
Even though the Great Pyramid
Is cool to see past noon.

The Sydney Opera House...
It's totally packed.
But we're running out of fuel,
And that's a fact!

The water at the Great Barrier Reef...
It is so blue.
Which country are we in?
I haven't a clue!

Let's turn around, Pete,
Before we're stuck.
In no man's land,
We'll be out of luck.

The Niagara Falls...
It's coming up.
Don't pet that
Rocky Mountain wolf pup.

Soon, we recognize some things
Like the Statue of Liberty.
After we turn the corner,
It's the Golden Gate Bridge I see.

We're flying fast,
And my face turns red.
Oh no! Is that a speed bump
That's up ahead?

We were lucky to get home,
That's for sure.
We both stopped farting,
And look much worse than before.

Why am I running?
It's not like she wants to wed.
I'd rather kiss her
Before I'm dead.

Fred...you still have a chance to flee...

Printed in the USA
CPSIA information can be obtained
at www.ICGtesting.com
LVHW061544130124
768647LV00022B/1369